Mysterious Somerset

Bossiney Books • Launceston

Some other Bossiney titles which may be of interest
About Glastonbury by Polly Lloyd
Ghosts of Somerset by Peter Underwood
Ghost hunting South-West by Michael Williams
King Arthur: man or myth? by Paul White
King Arthur's footsteps by Paul White
Psychic phenomena of the West by Michael Williams
Spiritual guides in the West Country by Jane White
Visions of Glastonbury by Ian Pethers

Published 2003 by Bossiney Books Ltd,
Langore, Launceston, Cornwall PL15 8LD
www.bossineybooks.co.uk
© 2003 Bossiney Books Ltd
ISBN 1-899383-59-X
Printed in Great Britain by R Booth (Troutbeck Press), Mabe, Cornwall

Hauntings

Michael Williams

The ghosts of Somerset are various and numerous.

Many of them 'inhabit' ancient locations like churches and pubs – old buildings have often been scarred by history. If we take churches, for example, centuries of prayers have been offered up within their walls. There is also a school of thought that many of our churches stand on former pagan sites and on ley lines – all of which could increase their potential for supernatural manifestation. Or if we consider the inns of the county, there are centuries of living and enjoyment within these convivial places.

Some psychic investigators also believe there is a connection between ghosts and stone. They believe that, in some curious way, the stone can somehow absorb 'emanations' from people, especially in stressful times, and store them as we might store vision on film or sound on tape. On occasion that stored 'information' is replayed – all of which gets us back to why when we enter an old building we may get an impression of happiness or depression.

I have always been interested in the fact that the majority of British ghosts are phantom women. This may not be surprising when we discover that statistically there are fewer men in the country – and always have been. I have another theory. Having interviewed hundreds of people claiming supernatural experience, I know that most of them were women. Men fearing scorn and ridicule perhaps?

Somerset certainly has her share of 'ladies'.

The Theatre Royal at Bath has a Grey Lady who occasionally sits in a box above the audience – some say she threw herself to her death. Then at Crowcombe there have been reports of a 'lady in blue' seen in the Rectory.

There have been other accounts of phantom white ladies seen standing guard over bridges and trackways. The White Lady of Wellow, though, was no guardian spirit, for it was said her rare appearance was supposed to 'announce' a death in the Hungerford family.

Witches, too, punctuate Somerset history. One such character, Jane Brooks, who hailed from Shepton Mallet, bewitched a twelve-year-old boy by offering him 'a bite of a magical apple'. The unfortunate lad immediately became airborne, finally crash-landing on the doorstep of a house. Jane Brooks was charged with witchcraft, found guilty and duly hanged at Chard.

In 1680 a man was tried at Taunton Assizes for witchcraft and acquitted by a sympathetic judge. Suddenly an old woman cried out from the courtroom: 'God bless your Lordship! ... Forty years ago they would have hanged me for a witch and they could not, and now they would have hanged my poor son.'

Here in the west country we are in Celtic territory where the worship of the spirits of water once held great significance. Pins were dropped into wells, and unspoken wishes made. Time was when there were two types of well: the wishing well and the cursing well. The latter were much in evidence until the early 1800s when they were filled in after being regarded as 'unsavoury relics of pagan superstition'.

Against this kind of background Somerset is natural ghost hunting country, but I must not give the impression of all local ghosts being wicked – or even frightening. Indeed some of the Somerset sightings have been so solid, so life-like, that the realisation has only struck the observer later – say when the figure has inexplicably vanished. Discovering the identity of a ghost, of course, can be an interesting challenge. For instance, the ghost of Forde Abbey, south west of Chard, is thought to be that of Thomas Chard who was Abbot of the Cistercian establishment at the Dissolution. When the ghost has been seen there, he is normally standing by the table in the great hall, gazing about the place he loved in his lifetime.

The identity of 'the Spanish traveller' murdered at the Plough Hotel, Holford, in 1555, however, remains a mystery. Was he a spy? Was a rich traveller killed for his money? Who was he? We shall probably never know the answers but James Westworth Day and Peter Underwood, two eminent ghost writers and hunters, have written of 'a dark clothed figure' seen at the Plough.

And more hauntings

Lornie Leete-Hodge

There are many tales surrounding the Arthurian legend, but this one concerns the villages of West and Queen Camel where, to the north, are traces of a causeway. Best seen when the spring grass is growing or from the air, it is the track along which Arthur is said to ride out at the head of his knights on Midsummer's Eve. What a wonderful sight!

A phantom of a much later king, Henry II, is also connected with this area. A visitor in the early 1920s was surprised to see standing in a field a large house which she had not noticed on previous walks. As a stranger, she saw nothing abnormal in the house, though it looked both solid and very old, and she paid little heed.

Then she noticed a man and a small boy standing by the door and was struck by their unusual clothes. They seemed to be staring straight at her. She stood still wondering whether to speak to them, and both the house and the figures disappeared. One moment they were facing her – the next they had gone.

She made enquiries, but no trace of a house could be discovered. It was later learned that Prince Henry lived in Somerset as a child, in hiding as a safety precaution during the wars between

King Stephen and Matilda, and the exact location was a well-kept secret. So the woman probably saw the ghosts of the young prince and his guardian.

Near Blagdon in the Blackdown hills there is said to be an earth spirit nicknamed Charlie. He sits on the clavey or beam above the fireplace in houses, and is made of holman or holly.

One evening a farmer was giving a dinner party. He had once poured scorn on Charlie and, unluckily for him, Charlie remembered. When the guests assembled, they found the table bare, the silver put away and the tankards hung up and empty. All the food and drink had disappeared. This was a sure sign that Charlie did not approve. The dinner was cancelled.

Stogumber, a village in the Brendon Hills, is set in an agricultural area where hunting has been a favourite sport over the centuries since Cardinal Beaufort, then the wealthiest man in England, hunted here after the church was built in medieval times. Combe Sydenham, two miles away, was the seat of the Sydenham family, one of whom married Sir Francis Drake. Legend claims that a meteorite, preserved there in the family home, and allegedly fired by Sir Francis from the Spanish Main, prevented his bride marrying a rival. Some think that if it is removed, it will always return.

The white, ghostly figure of Sir George Sydenham – father of the bride – is said to ride down the combe every night between midnight and cockcrow on a headless grey horse, but it is the Wild Hunt which provide the most spectacular haunting as they ride through the streets with trotting horses, bridles a-jingle, and baying hounds. When they rode through as late as the 1960s no one dared to look out as they heard the sounds!

In the 19th century a local ploughboy went to Rodhuish to have a plough blade mended. At the smithy, talk turned to the Croydon Hill Devil, a horned beast said to lurk in a lane over the hill. The butcher's boy thought he would scare the other lad by

5

waylaying him and imitating the Devil. As the ploughboy approached the lane on his way home, a dreadful monster charged at him, bellowing furiously. In his terror, he lashed out with the ploughblade and fled. All that was later found was a bullock's hide with a great gash in it and some horns, but the butcher boy was never seen again. It was believed the Devil had taken him. He can be heard howling on Croydon Hill on stormy nights when his and other lost souls are hounded by demons.

Minehead, a lovely seaside resort on the Bristol Channel's southern coast, is bounded on one side by the sea and at its rear by the thickly wooded steep and deep valleys of the northern fringes of Exmoor. Its harbour has been a haven for shipping over the centuries, and its situation in the shelter of towering North Hill ensures protection from the strong coastal winds. But all has not always been plain sailing.

In the 17th century, Mrs Leakey was a woman beloved by all in Minehead. When she died, her spirit underwent a terrible change, attacking travellers on lonely roads, conjuring up storms at sea and sinking ships, and everyone was in despair. Exorcism was tried but only made matters worse and provoked more violence. Charles I sent a Royal Commission to investigate, and at long last a bishop quelled the terrible phantom. Mrs Leakey's powers may have diminished, but beware of the Culver Cliffs where she is said to haunt still!

In the 18th century a prosperous innkeeper lived in Shepton Mallet by the name of Giles Cannard. He owed much of his wealth to dealings with smugglers, sheep stealers and highwaymen, and became involved in a plan to defraud the town of its common land. The news leaked out to the fury of the townsfolk who marched to his inn with murder in their hearts.

Terrified, Giles hanged himself and was buried at the crossroads with a stake in his heart to prevent him from walking. All to no avail, and soon he was seen near his old inn – long since

6

vanished – and near the crossroads where he was buried. There is a pub nearby called Cannard's Grave which had the sign of a corpse hanging from the gallows, its creaking making an eerie sound. One version claims that Cannard was the last man in England hanged for sheep stealing, but whichever is true, he is still restless.

Around the Quantocks are said to be many apparitions. At Weacombe a ghostly dog, evidently friendly, leads those who are lost to safety, and the road from St Audrie's Farm to Perry Farm has a Black Dog. No one thinks this one is friendly, and the area has other oddities in the shape of a coffin lying in the road and a 'grey, shapeless thing'. Maybe it has escaped from the coffin!

At Staple there is a belief that an old woman known as the 'Woman of the Mist' haunts the hills, and a solicitor alleged she appeared to him carrying a bundle of sticks.

Stogursey has claim to both black dogs and witches. This village derives its name from the Norman family of De Courcey who had a castle which was destroyed during the Wars of the Roses. The church was originally a Benedictine priory and has some fantastic carvings. Nearby is Wick Barrow, once believed to be the burial place of Hubba, a Dane, but later proved to be a Bronze Age Barrow.

Pixies have long been associated with the mound. A ploughman working nearby heard the sound of a child crying, complaining that it had broken its peel – a wooden shovel for putting loaves in an oven. The ploughman found a tiny wooden peel, its handle broken. He thought the childish owner was hiding in some bushes and would return for its toy, so he mended it and left it where it had lain. When his ploughing was done, he returned to find the peel gone, and in its place a cake, hot from the pixie's oven. The child's cries can still be heard, but no one else has had a cake.

Red-clothed fairies were said to have last been seen at

Buckland St Mary where they were defeated in a pitched battle with the Pixies. Afterwards the land was called Pixyland. The fairies' faint cries can be heard by those with good ears, and the pixies recognised by their red hair, pointed ears and preference for green!

In spite of long religious links and peaceful existence, a witch was supposed to live at Stogursey, who, if annoyed, would cast a spell powerful enough to overturn carts as they passed. And a large black dog casts a malevolent eye on people, often jumping out at them unawares. No one dares ask the name of his owner...

Muchelney Abbey, a Benedictine monastery standing in the Somerset wetlands, must have given its pious inhabitants rheumatism, but the area also produced many eels so there was no shortage of food in Lent. The Abbey was Saxon in foundation and, though long gone, many of its stones are incorporated into other buildings nearby.

In its heyday, the abbey provided the setting for a sad, haunting tale. A penniless young man fell in love with the daughter of a wealthy knight who forbade their marriage. In desperation the luckless suitor became a monk and later Prior of Muchelney. There to his joy and surprise he found his love who, in her misery, had become a nun. Their love rekindled, they planned to elope, but were overheard and their secret betrayed. He was sent to a distant monastery, but the poor nun, lurking in wait for her lover in a secret passage, was walled up alive. Her ghost is said to beg for release and his voice echo to her from afar that he is coming.

Crewkerne and Chard lie in the south of the county towards the Dorset border, with the Axe rippling below. Crewkerne was known for its canvas trade, and made much of the sailcloth for the fleets that sailed to defeat Napoleon. Chard is an ancient town of Saxon origin, almost totally destroyed in a terrible fire in 1577, allowing for imaginative and attractive rebuilding. The cloth trade flourished here, with gloves and lace as well, and its streams meander to the Bristol and English Channels.

Both places are busy, industrious and peaceful, yet the main road between them is said to be haunted by a phantom fight. Horses are heard galloping desperately, and a fight has been witnessed between smugglers and Revenue men. A wounded customs officer can be heard gasping for breath.

The west country has strong connections with the murder of Thomas à Becket, as all four of the knights who killed him were from that area. In a silent remote corner there is a lonely place which stands as a constant reminder of Thomas's martyrdom, for here are the remains of Woodspring Priory, once a religious establishment founded forty years after the murder by William de Courtenay, grandson of one of the perpetrators of the deed, Sir William de Tracy. He actually came from Devon and tried to sail to the Holy Land to expiate his crime.

The people recited the rhyme, 'The Tracys, the Tracys, the wind in their faces', to remind them, and fishermen were said to hear his voice wailing in the night winds. Others believe that Reginald Fitzurse, born at Williton, founded the priory and during the three hundred years of its existence, its land ownership was extended by gifts from the relatives of the murderers.

Two of the murdering knights were buried in unhallowed ground on the island of Flat Holm, facing north according to legend. One of them, Sir William de Tracy, is said to utter cries of anguish as he tries to make bundles of sand bound with rope, and the curse laid on his family remains.

The ruins remain of an old infirmary erected in the 19th century as an isolation ward for sailors with cholera; it had a crematorium attached. In October 1900 the remains of a sailor believed to have died of bubonic plague were burned there. Maybe his ghost lends song to the others in that lonely, eerie island. The priory still stands like a sentinel, silent witness to the past with an air of sadness and deep haunting.

Strange sightings and mystical paths

Rosemary Clinch

What was it a service engineer saw while he was driving his car down Chard High Street in 1975? It was 8 am on a February morning and no doubt reasonably light for the time of year, when suddenly his thoughts were interrupted. He caught sight of what resembled a huge bird with a wing span of 12-14 ft (3.5-4 m). Passing briefly overhead it went out of sight over shops and houses in a matter of seconds.

No doubt he pondered on this experience for days.

What are UFOs? Are there such things as 'flying saucers' and ships shaped like long cigars containing smaller 'scout' vehicles? Are they really ice particles or space debris as scientists and astronomers explain or are they just clouds assuming strange shapes under certain weather conditions?

It could be said that to believe in ghosts is to accept something outside our physical world. If we can accept visitors from the past, why not from the future too, and why not outside our own solar system? Strange sightings go back to ancient times with reports of flying chariots, the sun dropping below the clouds, and 'magic' weapons in Celtic days when whole armies were wiped out by flames.

Legends also tell of giants buried in long barrows; some say skeletons 8 ft or more (2.5 m) have been found within these mounds. Could this be the reason many of the barrows carry the name 'giant', such as Giant's Grave at Holcombe, and could the bones have been the remains of settlers here from outer space?

People seeking answers to the UFO enigma have noted the

similarity of the shape of barrows to the objects sighted in our skies – barrows have long been given the descriptive names of 'disc', 'bell' and 'saucer'.

Reported sightings in recent years have more often consisted of shining silver discs, 'mother' ships, silver crosses and clusters of lights, very often moving at incredible speeds, faster than any aircraft made by humans.

Misunderstandings often happen and although it can be said that scientists and astronomers do not generally believe in UFOs, they do keep an open mind. This is what a Weston-super-Mare astronomer did when he was making his usual observations with binoculars one night. Suddenly, he saw a brilliant white light approaching him from the south at a phenomenal speed. Astonished, he watched it perform a sharp right-angle and double back on itself – at a speed no aircraft would be capable of.

Then it revealed itself for what it was – a white owl! The astronomer's natural curiosity as to the reasons for this effect found that this UFO appearance could be put down to the high sodium lighting content in that particular area of the town reflecting on the bird's feathers!

Not so easily explained are one or two sightings experienced in the Bath area and reported in the local newspaper at the time. In 1982 in Bath, a salesman saw a large incandescent ball travelling slowly towards Box in Wiltshire at about 3000 ft (900 m). He could only describe the object as totally alien and reported it to the RAF. No explanation ensued from this encounter, but the Ministry of Defence took the matter seriously enough to ask him for a statement.

Again near Bath, in Lower Weston, a husband and wife were going to bed early one Sunday night in 1978. As they lay facing the window, a tremendous orange glow came round the side of the curtain. Tentatively they watched as it was followed by an orange object shaped like a tear-drop lying on its side with a tapered tail. There was no sound as it moved very fast in fifteen seconds across the night-gathering sky, turning from orange to ordinary light.

Bath seems to have had a predominance of glowing orange sightings, but one couple had an even closer encounter one evening between Bath and Melksham. They were following a ring of lights which they took to be planes flying in formation, but it was moving unusually slowly and their car eventually caught up. As they looked up underneath the object, they saw two rings of multi-coloured lights. There was no noise. It was a clear night and the object was 400 to 500 ft (120-150 m) up and about 50 ft (15 m) in diameter, with its lights slowly going on and off! A strange experience for what must be said were very sane and intelligent people.

In 1979 many people in Somerset, including a helicopter pilot at the Royal Naval Air Station in Yeovilton, saw an orange disc. This actually set off a spate of 999 calls from Aberdeen in Scotland to Wales. It was estimated to be travelling at about 1500 mph (2400 km/h) but, on investigation, Jodrell Bank reported it was certainly space debris.

To read Von Däniken's experiences and theories stirs the imagination, despite many criticisms and accusations of misinterpretation, but the evidence for UFOs cannot easily be dismissed. Probably all of us have seen something in the skies which cannot be identified and yet is casually ignored.

Unseen and even more obscure than UFOs in their fascination are ley lines, marked only for the 'ley hunter', by linking anything which is old and spiritually or otherwise sacred so that it forms a straight line on an Ordnance Survey map. There is a theory that UFOs possibly use these lines for navigation by tapping the magnetic power they are purported to contain. This is very difficult to prove but it is not difficult to prove the existence of lines which appear to criss-cross the country from one ancient site to another.

Who was the originator of this theory? As a safe local dignitary in Herefordshire in the 1920s, Alfred Watkins was aware of the effect of any socially unacceptable theory. The archaeological world was outraged when, in his late sixties, he finally decided to reveal his findings while roaming through the countryside with leisured and retired members of a naturalists' field club, typical of many to be found in those days.

Early people placed great importance on the way they positioned stone and had an obvious obsession with mathematics and geometry. But how did they do it, and is this perhaps another link with UFOs and help from elsewhere? Could it be that since early man and his possible use of ley lines for spiritual power, their purpose has just simply been forgotten?

Leys pass through many megalithic stones and some people have experienced sensations of shock or trembling when touching them, suggesting they are a power source. Identified by the name of 'the Living Rock' are the fragments of an old megalith on the western slopes of Glastonbury Tor. It has been found that these large fragments emit mild shock waves if touched early in the morning or late in the evening!

Enfolded by mysticism, Glastonbury is the centre of a diverse range of religious customs and followings – it is said that Joseph of Arimathea brought the infant Jesus here and that the famous Holy Thorn is descended from Joseph's staff which he stuck in the ground as they rested on Wearyall Hill. And for the ley hunter Glastonbury is a main source for ley lines fanning out in all directions. The abbey has the same geometrical plan as Stonehenge. Follow the line between the two and barrows, tumuli, earthworks, forts and churches can all be joined together.

The Cathedral at Wells is directly connected to Glastonbury Abbey by a ley which stretches westward to Castle Neroch near

Bridgwater. One of the oldest lines is the 'St Michael's Line' running from St Michael's Mount in Cornwall via Glastonbury Tor and the remains of St Michael's Church and on to Avebury in Wiltshire. Somerton also has a convergence of leys as well as Lamyatt at Lamyatt Beacon, the site of an ancient temple.

There is no overwhelming explanation why circles, tumuli and churches connect, but the evidence is they do and it is hard to understand the reluctance of archaeologists to accept this.

Anyone can prove it to themselves with a good straight ruler, well sharpened pencil and an Ordnance Survey map. Just simply look for an ancient site, tump, cairn or fort. Look for other similar sites including churches, Roman forts, beacon points or holy wells. Crossroads, ancient castles, islands and ponds are all likely candidates too – ring them all before taking the ruler to see if any of them connect.

The megalith-building people's reshaping of our landscape, with their movement of stones, has a lot to answer for. Maybe we know how they dragged the Bluestones for Stonehenge from Prescelly but we still strive to understand their minds and their motives. Maybe legends and folklore have the answers, intangible though they may be, and perhaps there is more to be learned from the ancient art of dowsing. The achievements of people 5000 years ago were strange enough to have warranted the use of forces beyond our knowledge today and it can only remain to be said, 'There are more things in heaven and earth…'

The self-styled Messiah

Ray Waddon

An eerie silence followed the lusty singing of a hymn by the well-dressed congregation in the white stone church, the 'Ark of the Covenant' in the then select north-east London suburb of Clapton.

One of the three beautiful stained-glass windows was suddenly darkened by a cloud on this memorable Sunday evening in early September 1902. It lent dramatic impact to an amazing pronouncement by a tall man in clerical attire.

Leading up to a semi-circular marble altar were richly carpeted steps. Beyond was a throne on which he was seated. Emaciated, of sallow countenance, he had dark glistening bright eyes. His thin black hair was parted down the centre of his small head.

Slowly he rose and stood looking fixedly at the many worshippers of both sexes. Then, speaking softly, almost musically, but with deliberation, he declared: 'I who speak to you tonight am that Lord Jesus Christ who died and rose again, and ascended into Heaven. I am that Lord Jesus, come again in my own body, to save those who come to me from death and judgment.'

The Reverend John Hugh Smyth-Pigott paused in his blasphemous staggering utterances, which were to make national and indeed international headlines. Gazing abstractly at his astounded hearers and raising his right hand, he said: 'It is not there, in Heaven, where you will find your God, but in me who am united with the Father.'

Slowly he walked back, sat down and buried his head in his hands. Silence again, broken this time by a woman crying: 'God is here! I see Him on the altar.'

'Behold! That is God,' said another.

A grey haired man rose, excitedly shouting: 'Behold! that is Christ!' One after another stood 'testifying to the Lord God' in emphatic penetrating tones. The entire body joined in singing to organ accompaniment 'Oh Hail Thou King of Glory'.

The wide publicity given in the press throughout the week, despite failure to interview Pigott, resulted in extraordinary scenes the following Sunday. For the morning service people had begun to take up positions before the locked gate of the church by six o'clock. Eventually about two hundred were admitted.

In clerical garb, and wearing a hat, Pigott's arrival in a two-horse brougham was the signal for hisses and booing. Inside he repeated his declaration of a week earlier that he was the new Messiah. Apart from a few interruptions the service passed off without incident.

Directly it was over there were wild and ugly scenes. By tram and brake, on cycle and on foot, an angry crowd numbering several thousand had gathered. Women moaned. Some fainted in the crush. Journalists were among the people swept aside in the mad rush. Police were unable to cope with the situation.

Reinforcements arrived, many of them mounted, but faced a hard task in efforts to control the noisy mob and protect Pigott from violence. Some of Pigott's flock tried to shield him and he was hustled into one of two waiting broughams. Fists were raised and insults hurled as, regardless of life and limb, the front driver whipped the horses into a gallop. It was little short of miraculous that Pigott reached his charming home, Cedar Lodge, by Clapton Common, unharmed.

The news in one of the national dailies of the mounted police escort to Cedar Lodge added that Pigott was going into retreat at a rural refuge in Somerset. This was the 'Agapemone' at Spaxton, 5 miles (8 km) west of Bridgwater.

However, to trace the events which brought Pigott to Somerset and linked him with another amazingly similar eccentric, it is necessary to go back to the end of the 19th century.

It was the Reverend Henry John Prince who had built the 'Ark of the Covenant' Church which Pigott had sensationalised. He also bought a mansion at Spaxton, naming it the Agapemone or 'Abode of Love' and founding a peculiar sect known as the Agapemonites.

Like Pigott, 'Brother Prince' was a Somerset man. Born at Bath, he studied medicine at Guy's Hospital, London. Ironically, ill health compelled him to give it up. Instead, he devoted himself to the Church, was ordained and given a curacy at Charlynch, a lovely little stone church dating from the 11th century, on a hill top a short distance from the Agapemone.

Prince's passion for young women was insatiable. Blasphemous ritual preceded his union with those with whom he chose to gratify his sexual desires, and he was unfrocked.

In 1899, to the utter astonishment of the wealthy coterie who had firmly believed this rogue when he proclaimed his own immortality, Prince went the way of all flesh. He was eighty-eight. At midnight, in secret, he was buried in the grounds. And 'upright' it was said, ready for the Resurrection.

Prince's secretary, Edwin Douglas Malcolm Hamilton, who came to live at the Abode when he was twenty-six, was thought to be a likely contender for the role of the new Messiah. A tall, broad-shouldered dour Scot, he had occupied a cottage in the large and well-kept grounds. Prince's rule had been that no male member should reside in the mansion itself. Fond of reading, Hamilton, a non-smoker and a vegetarian, was almost a hermit. He had promised the community he would search for a new 'Heavenly Bridegroom', apparently having no desire or intention to fulfil the exalted position.

It was in Dublin that Hamilton and Pigott met, though whether by design or accident is not clear. Hamilton persuaded him to proclaim himself the new Messiah, and some time after the Clapton sensation Pigott returned to his native county, this time as the Heavenly Bridegroom of the Agapemonites. He had told Hamilton to prepare a dossier of all the members, their interests and ages.

After perusing this carefully he wrote stating there were far too many old people there. Recruits, young and attractive, must be brought in. From overseas, he suggested.

When at length Hamilton had carried out these none-too-easy

instructions, Pigott's arrival at the Agapemone was heralded by the inmates being summoned to the luxuriously furnished chapel. There he once again declared himself to be the Son of Man.

Meanwhile Pigott had married. A devout member of the church, pretty auburn-haired Catherine Reynolds, fell in love with the young clergyman; she was entranced with his preaching and no doubt succumbed to his hypnotic influence.

When Pigott and his wife moved to the Agapemone, one account stated that they took with them a family friend, young vivacious Ruth Annie Preece. Another version is that suddenly, without any explanation as to how or where he found her, Pigott, who had been away for some time, brought the good-looking Ruth with him. But it was Ruth, and not the woman to whom he was lawfully wed, whom he installed as his Chief Soul Bride. And although his wife, Catherine, continued living at the Agapemone, it is certain that Ruth was the mother of his children.

This immoral conduct by Pigott aroused nation-wide publicity, and the Bishop of Bath and Wells, Dr Kennion, was determined that a citation should be served on him. It was extremely difficult to present personally the necessary legal documents. Two visits by the Bishop's secretary were abortive. 'The Messiah is away,' he was told. Eventually the complaint was served on 16 December 1908, and the Consistory Court took place about a month later at Wells Cathedral.

Outlining the case against Pigott, counsel for the Bishop referred to the uproar that had occurred at Clapton in 1902. 'Ruth Annie Preece,' he said, 'appeared to have become infatuated of Smyth-Pigott. She was one of the numerous women who attended services at that conventicle, and accompanied him to the Agapemone as his "spiritual wife" whatever that may mean.

'It is lamentable', counsel went on, 'that the defendant has been continuing the work of the notorious "Brother Prince" and converted, or continued to allow, the beautiful little hamlet of Spaxton to be a wilderness of particularly repulsive vices.'

Within a short time of the hearing, the Bishop intimated that Pigott was incapable of holding preferment in the Church on the grounds of immorality. In his absence, he was 'unfrocked'. His third child, a daughter, was born later.

It had long been said, both in Prince's day and in Pigott's, that the Agapemonites were very generous to the poor of the parish, especially at Christmas. Consequently it was not surprising when the people of Spaxton invariably declined to give any information about the Abode or its inhabitants to visiting pressmen. Offers of bribes were scorned.

Much on the same lines as his infamous predecessor, Pigott was always most careful in the choice of his female converts. That they should be of a pretty type, to satisfy his sensual demands, was coupled with their being wealthy. Their income, from whatever resources they possessed, had to be pooled. This was a strict order from him, the money being necessary to maintain the remarkable building, and for him and his favoured ones to live in luxury and free from any labours apart from hobbies, such as gardening, knitting, and playing croquet.

It was easy for journalists to describe the exterior of the Agapemone. Seen from a distance, it had the traditional outline of a church; but viewed at close quarters its appearance was entirely pagan.

There was a lantern tower with a lofty and delicate tapering spire. On the four top corners were almost life-sized figures of a bull, an eagle, a lion and a man – presumably representing an angel. The bull and the lion had wings, and the 'angel' knelt in a supplicating posture with one hand pointing to the sky.

Enclosed in towering walls almost as thick and high as those of a prison, the building and grounds were further safeguarded against prying eyes by massive solid oaken doors, studded with big nails. There was a resplendent lawn, well-kept and beautiful flower beds and greenhouses filled with exotic plants.

In addition to the main structure in which there were twenty bedrooms, banqueting hall, private apartments, and huge stone-flagged kitchens, several cottages provided excellent accommodation for some members. One was occupied by Hamilton, and others by the domestic staff, which included sixteen chambermaids.

The population of Bridgwater in Prince's early years at Spaxton was a mere twelve thousand. It was still very much the horse and carriage age for the affluent. Whisky was eighteen shillings a gallon, best cured ham cost seven pence a pound, and there was little in the way of entertainment.

It was therefore an exciting, and free, event when 'Brother Prince' made his occasional visits to the town to replenish supplies. Or maybe it was a form of self-gratification that caused him to make what were termed 'triumphant entries' in great splendour. The sight of four spanking bay horses drawing his carriage, with outrider postillion, and a number of bloodhounds alongside – at night they roamed the grounds – attracted much interest among the tradesmen and pedestrians.

In striking contrast, more than half a century later, Pigott's trips into town were commonplace. A writer in a Somerset newspaper in 1924 stated: 'The three children born to Pigott by his "spiritual bride" Sister Ruth have now grown up into bonny young people. Pigott is constantly motoring in the town, where his appearance now causes no excitement or interest.'

In the late twenties it was only on rare occasions that the Agapemone figured in the news. When it did the stories were mostly invented. The sect made it a rule to refuse any interviews; they lived in strict privacy.

Then suddenly it was front-page news again, at home and abroad. On Monday 21 March 1927, the *Chronicle* – which itself was to die three years later – had an exclusive story. Banner headlines on the front page read: 'Abode of Love loses its "Messiah"', 'Smyth-Pigott dies at the Agapemone', 'His soul wives', 'The Escapades of Sister Ruth'.

One of the very few photographs ever taken of Pigott was published. It had been taken near Taunton railway station, some twenty years earlier.

Fleet Street descended in force and the press invasion had reached its peak on the Thursday, to cover the funeral. At 10.30 a special squad of police arrived, among them a number of plain clothes officers. Some were placed on duty at the main entrance to the Agapemone. Others took up positions in the lane alongside the mansion.

More were at the rear, by way of fields and locked gates. A bloodhound joined in guarding the extensive grounds, barking ferociously.

In a field immediately opposite, on high ground, as an enthusiastic young reporter on a weekly newspaper, I attempted to climb a telegraph pole. Before I could catch even a glimpse of what was going on inside, a burly red-faced policeman hauled me down. Just as a personal memento I got a good snapshot with my small camera of one party in deep mourning entering on foot. I could identify only Pigott's family doctor and solicitor, both from Bridgwater.

To avoid breaking the law by causing an obstruction a *Daily Mirror* photographer instructed a Bridgwater taxi driver to go very slowly up and down the lane, repeatedly pausing by the huge doors. They were flung open by invisible hands each time a motorcar conveying mourners arrived. In the same mysterious manner they closed.

The intrepid cameraman was precariously perched on a pair of steps, on top of the Buick taxi. 'I've to be at Aintree tomorrow, for the Grand National,' he told me.

Spring had come to smiling Somerset. Lambs frisked and frolicked in the rich pasture land. The trees were beginning to unfurl their verdant green banners. Rooks were cawing busily about their nests.

The lane was now devoid of traffic. We of the press contingent agreed to maintain silence as we leant against the wall nearest the chapel. Floating across in the breeze the faint strains of the organ were an indication that the burial service was taking place; but in secrecy comparable with the forbidden Tibetan city of Lhasa. So the army of newspapermen and women could describe only the general scene, and resort to letting their pens run riot in highly coloured accounts.

'A time to be born and a time to die,' says Ecclesiastes. The mortal remains of Spaxton's second self-acclaimed Messiah lay in a village-made coffin, covered by the rich red soil of the Quantock Hills country.

Would it mean that the curtain was now being run down for ever at the peaceful home of this declining and ageing sect? Occasionally if some new angle could be found they would be revived in the cold print of the more sensation-loving Sunday newspapers.

Sister Ruth, who had changed her name to Smyth, was understood to be the principal. Hamilton apparently had no desire to become the new leader.

One event in 1936 was productive of an item that served an opportunity of rehashing some of the history of the place. This was the death, and secret burial, of Catherine Smyth-Pigott, the 'lawful' widow. She was aged eighty-five, and had been in failing health for a considerable time. Throughout she had been devoted to Ruth, and was much liked by all the residents and the villagers who counted it a privilege to know her.

However, the long and so often sensationalised life of the Abode of Love, which might better have borne the title the

Abode of Free Love, with its ritual and closely-guarded secrets, entered its final stages when Sister Ruth died.

There was now no need for esotery. The real life drama of supposed celestial happiness on the earthly plane reached a climax the week after Easter in 1956. The seclusion was relaxed at last. Not only were villagers and friends in the neighbourhood admitted to the wonderful chapel but representatives of the press for the funeral service – the press which over the years had ruthlessly pilloried the Agapemonites, taking full advantage of their rigid refusal to grant interviews, and in consequence publishing columns of hocus-pocus and hyperbole.

For the first time and at very short notice we were able to see and to take photographs of the 'place of worship'. The strident notes of the magnificent organ, one of the finest in the country, greeted us on entering. The pungent aroma of incense filled our nostrils.

Shrouded in black against the east wall stood the altar, furnished with a cross and two highly polished brass candlesticks. The tall white candles were lighted as mourners arrived. The coffin, resting on trestles draped with golden coloured fabric, was adorned with a mass of spring flowers, with trumpet daffodils predominating. The open grave lay before the altar. The sanctuary was reached by a flight of four steps running the width of the chapel. Above the altar hung two large pastoral scenes in oil, painted by members of the community. On one side was the Madonna and Child; on the other a large framed photograph of the 'Ark of the Covenant' church.

Sister Ruth's two sons and daughter were the chief mourners. Agapemonites aged from upwards of seventy to ninety-four, with a few retainers, sat on the right. A number of parishioners and we 'scribes' sat on a higher level at the rear.

A colleague looked around, turned and whispered guilefully, 'We weren't so very far out in our description!'

It was a solemn and intensely impressive service. Yet it served as a reminder of the heresy and hypocrisy that had been enacted within its walls from the aspidistra age of Victoriana until, at least, the late 1920s.

After the opening sentences, the Archbishop of Karin, of the Catholic Apostolic Church of the Good Shepherd, Chelsea, the Most Reverend H P Nicholson, DD, announced that, at the request of the late Mrs Smyth and the community, he had the previous evening consecrated the chapel and its grounds.

Wearing cassock, surplice, and a purple skull cap, he kissed the sons and daughter. His chaplain, the Reverend Paul Craft, in cassock and surplice, swung the thurible while the Archbishop sprinkled holy water over the coffin.

In the spring of 1962 the impenetrable curtain on the whole place finally fell. The property was sold. So numerous were the sightseers that the lane was completely blocked. Cars and the Saturday afternoon bus to town were held up.

Later in the year the organ was dismantled by a well-known Taunton firm of organ builders and removed to the Roman Catholic Church of the Holy Cross at Bedminster, Bristol.

What was to become of the chapel, the reputed centre of a disorderly house; a den of corruption yet a dignified structure of architectural merit and historic interest? The family, who had survived Pigott, happily and generously refused to allow it to be bulldozed in the name of 'progress' and so suffer the fate of many buildings of note.

The local authority, Bridgwater Rural District Council, gave planning permission for its conversion into a puppet studio. The purchasers were genial Bob Bura, an ENSA entertainer in the war, and his partner, young, tall John Hardwick – both London born but lovers of rural England.

Together this highly talented couple transformed the chapel to meet the requirements of their unusual and very technical profession, stop motion animation.

Some while after the funeral of Sister Ruth, I visited the former chapel to have a chat with Bob and John. It was pleasing to find that the lovely parquet floor and striking lancet windows had been retained. Gone of course, were the altar, the pastoral scenes, and the organ.

At irregular intervals, over a period covering six reigns, the Boer War and two world wars, a peaceful rural parish had suffered the dubious distinction of having the spotlight of the nation on it. The story had been seized on by the sensational sections of the press as first-class copy to be devoured by the masses.

One redeeming feature was that the major events took place before the age of television. Otherwise, the courteous hardworking Spaxtonians would have been subjected to the ignominy of being forced to appear on the screens in millions of homes. The outbreak of the Second World War meant that the Agapemonites were of little interest to Fleet Street, and in 1942 not much publicity was given to the death of Hamilton, who had been secretary to both Prince and Pigott.

The parallel in the lives of these two renegade eccentrics was that both were ordained in the Church of England, unfrocked for immoral conduct, lived in luxury in a secluded harem, and claimed to be the Redeemer and Saviour of mankind.

King Arthur?

Michael Williams

Psycho-expansion is a technique which enables individuals to explore and develop their sense of awareness. The claim is the mind is therefore able to move in time and space. In a sentence: it is time travel.

Personally I have not undergone psycho-expansion, but I have spoken to people in a state of regression – travelling back to an earlier life or lives. The idea of reincarnation is a fascinating one; some people and cultures accept it easily, whereas others are more sceptical.

I have interviewed a west country housewife on several occasions who claims she was King Arthur in a former life. She sees nothing strange or inconsistent in that once she was a man. 'Some people come back to this life many times,' she explained, 'and in very different forms... there seem to be no rules, save those of cause and effect.'

During these interviews I have been impressed by the variety of changes in her personality. In regression, for example, she sits differently; her voice becomes noticeably lower in key. Listening to this Aquarian lady you are aware that she is giving a kind of commentary, but no matter-of-fact commentary, no plateau of emotion. At times she is genuinely troubled, and other times highly amused. You are forced to one of two conclusions: she is either a very talented actress (as far as I know she has never been on the stage) or you are watching and listening to something not quite of this world.

The following is an account of one of our conversations.

Question: What makes you so sure that Arthur belongs to reality?

Answer: The name Arthur is really a kind of family name, a title describing a hereditary role which involves some type of leadership. I know that the Arthur who lived in the west country during the period 451-518 AD belongs to my reality through my past lives research over many years.

When I first recalled this life, I had no idea who he was until one group session of psycho-expansion some months later, when I was questioned. During psycho-expansion we relax into a state of heightened consciousness, the alpha state. Briefly, the brain has two halves: the left is the analytical side, while the right observes patterns and colours, and is intuitive. The tendency is to rely too much on the left in modern life. Generally, I believe we are not realising our full potential. Through this shift in the level of consciousness you become more aware, more perceptive, rather like tuning in to your own mind computer.

I was asked who I was and I 'heard' myself saying that I was a Celtic tribal leader, giving a Celtic name which roughly translated means 'who is of fire'. With the recall of other members of the psycho-expansion groups who did their research at different sessions, we gradually realised that many of us had been together before and lots of the information we got individually we confirmed with each other later on. So many people 'saw' me, and I 'saw' many of the others. It was quite an extraordinary time, checking this information. The discovery of my apparent life as Arthur, Artos, which is a very honest and real, albeit at times quite shattering experience to me, is only one of my many other apparent lives... some very ordinary and others extraordinary.

Question: Do you think proof will one day emerge confirming, once and for all, that Arthur is a genuine historical figure?

Answer: I'm not sure what sort of proof can really confirm to the general public that Arthur existed, apart from some artefact or piece of writing with his name on it! However, I'm sure that if we need some type of proof it will be revealed when the time is right. As far as Arthur being a genuinely historical figure, I can only say that we have found this person, his family and his connections operating in what is known historically as the Dark Ages in Britain, with the strongest links in the west country. So far, I haven't discovered him in the north and I wonder if there was another leader who was an 'Arthur' operating there at this time. The place names incorporating Arthur abound all over the country, which I find an intriguing point.

Question: Though you and I have talked about your earlier life, we've not really discussed the others. What was Merlin's influence? What kind of woman was Guinevere? What was the atmosphere of Camelot? Was Excalibur a magical sword?

Answer: Merlin's influence – or the person we call Merlin (since one of his roles in those times was Bishop Merlinus) – was considerable. He was in fact the father of Arthur. He was a very wise man with considerable knowledge of the ancient religion, but he spent a lot of his time in travelling, particularly in Brittany where there were strong family connections.

Merlin arranged for Arthur's upbringing as a warrior from a very early age with a great deal of Roman influence. He also acted as a mediator between the tribes, bringing them together in order that there should be more of a united front when the invasions began to develop more seriously. He advised Arthur on many matters – sometimes with difficulty – since Arthur was a bit headstrong, especially in his younger years.

Guinevere – the name was rather different then – was betrothed to Arthur when he was quite young, around the age of fifteen or sixteen. He went through a ceremony in Brittany where there was a great gathering of tribes at Carnac. Attached to this ceremony was his taking on formally of some kind of responsibility as a leader – a dedication, I think.

I'm not quite sure how Guinevere fits into my recall, except she didn't return to Britain with Arthur at that time. This was an arranged betrothal, as so many seemed to be in those days, to establish the links with family and tribes. There seemed to be a lot of inter-marrying and everyone seemed quite happy with these arrangements. I 'remember' her as having very fair hair – just a girl – but from an important family. She had a child, a son, and they came to Dorset first and then Somerset when the boy was about two years old.

I am not sure about Camelot. The word never brings me any 'far memory'. However, if I 'ask' about Cadbury Castle I get an immediate response as being a very important place for Arthur which he used as a great fortress, having caused it to be strengthened and developed to contain whole tribes. I have never visited it in this life so far except through 'mind' research. This reveals a strong ley line connecting it with Glastonbury which seems to continue up and around into the Severn area and the Forest of Dean where Arthur also had connections. The name Caerleon also gives me a very strong reaction.

The sword Excalibur I discovered was a very special sword which manifested at Avebury. When I was doing this piece of research, I was quite amazed and reluctant to give the details of what happened – it's far too much like something out of a film! However, suffice it to say that I now understand that Excalibur is a symbol of great strength and protection which may appear to anyone – perhaps in meditation, where there is a particularly strong need which involves mankind.

Question: Can you give us a word picture of the Somerset of your day?

Answer: The Somerset of Arthur's day was extremely beautiful – such forests of trees… There seemed to be a great deal more water, first of all coming in on the sea coast not far from Minehead and of course all around Glastonbury Tor. During this lifetime of Arthur I seemed to be mainly travelling on two routes – one was all along the northern coasts of the west country, and the other was into Dorset. I think Somerset was really the centre of Arthur's activities, or perhaps he always seemed to be returning there. It was such a fragrant area – or may be the senses were sharper in the people of those times. What always struck me when 'mind travelling' were the great number of trees everywhere.

Question: Why do you think Somerset is such a mysterious place? I put that question to you as Arthur and to you as you are now. It's interesting that you spent part of this life living in Somerset.

Answer: I wonder if Arthur thought that Somerset was a mysterious place. He was certainly aware that it was served by a great ley line and that Glastonbury was a very 'energised' place.

By this I mean that the force field in the vicinity of the Tor was exceptional – it was enhanced. This effect draws one back to a place because the atmosphere is rarefied – an excellent healing centre. He had occasion to seek help there for many of his wounds sustained in battle.

I still think Somerset has an air of mystery about it, but like most counties you have to get off the main roads to 'feel' it. When I lived in Somerset as a child I was fortunate in having the opportunity to accompany my father in his car when he had to visit many farms in the course of his work.

Looking back, I'm so glad to have experienced those journeys by road and lane with little traffic about, and to be able to explore the country churches. It truly is a county of many contrasts with its levels and great protecting hills. We had moved from Surrey and my lasting memory of Somerset is always as the county of the meadowsweet growing in great clumps everywhere, but especially heady and fragrant near the canals. For all our outings around the country places the one place my father and I never visited was Glastonbury!

So, I had no preconceived ideas about this area when over thirty years later I was exploring it through the technique of psycho-expansion and mind travel, and making notes of my findings and feelings as a tribal leader in the 5th century AD. I did finally get there in this life and found it difficult to cope with the different layers of occupation since Celtic times. I have still not climbed the Tor itself, yet I can very easily go back to being in Arthur's body and recall the view. I must return just for old time's sake!

Question: I think you, as you are now, had a strange experience in Somerset. Can you tell me about it?

Answer: My eldest daughter married, and she and her husband moved to a house near Williton, Somerset. A year later, I was visiting them and unfortunately strained my back. Sitting in her living room, I could see the church tower on the horizon and my intuition moved me (very gingerly!) to get into my car to discover the reason why I must go.

On arrival, I explored the church – St Decuman's – which was very well kept, and then the grounds where I found a little path sloping down to a garden and, I think, a well. This garden had been lovingly created out of a wilderness, I believe, but the sense of peace within it suddenly overwhelmed me. Then I felt a strong line of energy behind me as I descended the path with halting steps – due to my back condition. I stepped sideways and found it less distinguishable, so I positioned myself again and stood still, allowing my back to be against the flow. Some ten minutes later I turned to climb back up the garden path with the realisation that my steps were now unfaltering – there was only the slightest twinge in my back!

I reached my car and this time there was no need to ease myself into the driving seat and when I returned to my daughter, demonstrating how much better my back was, all she said was, 'You're mad, mother!' At that time, as you will have gathered, she was not 'into all that stuff', her own words for that which isn't obvious! She has since learned differently for herself, which is important. Learning about your intuition and ultimately trusting it is probably the most important step in self-discovery. Anyway, I went on to enjoy the rest of my stay thanks to my intuition and Mother Earth's healing energies. Others may wonder if St Decuman had a hand in it!

Question: Finally, as you believe in reincarnation, do you think

Arthur will reappear one day in his Arthurian form?

Answer: For me, reincarnation appears to be obvious due to my own experiences of past lives and many years of research, so when you ask me if I think Arthur will reappear one day in his Arthurian form I can only reply by saying that, if he did, would he be recognised?

The Arthur that I found myself to be as a tribal leader in the 5th century was only a part of an intricate story which somehow captured the headlines of the day as an idea and was passed on through myth and legend to describe the journey that we undertake through a physical life. The story and the idea still survive because the pitfalls, the decisions, the courageous acts and the romances are what we all experience in a lifetime. We all have a quest, whether it be in a material sense or a spiritual one – it just depends on how enquiring your nature is and what your intent is, as well as how your inner needs must be met. So I believe we are all Arthurs, or part of his idea right now, whether we are men, women or children.

The discovery of my own incarnation has led me to understand that a soul may be called on at any time to fulfil a particular leadership role. My own role as the fifth-century Arthur was certainly in defending his people at a critical time, but it was his love of the land in which he found himself operating that was important to him. We face a similar threat now, but on a global scale. Our desire for swift evolution has polluted the land which supports us – the planet Earth – so we have become our own worst enemies.

Will Arthur reappear in his Arthurian form? I think he already has – in each one of us. How must we Arthurs respond in saving our lands, our planet? Many of the answers lie hidden in myth and legend.